T0047242

THE LEETER
SPIAKING SINGLISH
2

THE LEETER
SPIᴀKING
SINGLISH

BOOK 2:
IDIOMS

Gwee Li Sui

mc Marshall Cavendish
Editions

Published in 2022 by Marshall Cavendish Editions
An imprint of Marshall Cavendish International

Other Marshall Cavendish Offices:
Marshall Cavendish Corporation, 800 Westchester Ave, Suite N-641, Rye Brook, NY 10573, USA • Marshall Cavendish International (Thailand) Co Ltd, 253 Asoke, 16th Floor, Sukhumvit 21 Road, Klongtoey Nua, Wattana, Bangkok 10110, Thailand • Marshall Cavendish (Malaysia) Sdn Bhd, Times Subang, Lot 46, Subang Hi-Tech Industrial Park, Batu Tiga, 40000 Shah Alam, Selangor Darul Ehsan, Malaysia

Marshall Cavendish is a registered trademark of Times Publishing Limited

National Library Board, Singapore Cataloguing in Publication Data

Name(s): Gwee, Li Sui, 1970-
Title: The Leeter Spiaking Singlish. Book 2, Idioms / Gwee Li Sui.
Description: Singapore : Marshall Cavendish Editions, 2022.
Identifier(s): ISBN 978-981-5009-61-3
Subject(s): LCSH: English language--Variation--Singapore. | English language--Spoken English--Singapore. | English language--Dialects--Singapore.
Classification: DDC 427.95957--dc23

Printed in Singapore

CONTENTS

TERIMA KASIH!

SINGAPORE GOT a lot of wonderful non-Singlish speakers. My lao bu is one of them. She does not even know what is Singlish – which is sikit awkward for me, the supposed big Singlish guy. But my lao bu oso cannot spiak England and Mandarin, two of our national languages I got go school to learn. Nonid to even talk about her Melayu and Tamil. She is spiak Teochew nia.

Because socially I must England and Mandarin while my lao bu can only Teochew, I end up discovering Singlish. Because my lao bu cannot make sense of much else, let alone code-switch, unker must chum siong and rojak my Teochew with England, Mandarin, and simi stray words she knows. This must be happening to many relationships across Singapore or how can Singlish be so diverse and kuat?

So Book Two of *The Leeter Spiaking Singlish* is dedicate to Madam Soh Hwee Noil and hampalang Sinkies who can spiak one way nia. Because of them and we who sayang them, there can continue to be Singlish. Sometimes, when I hear peepur say Singlish speakers need to think of those who cannot code-switch, unker wans to reply, "Acherly, we think of them all the time."

INTRODUCTION

IF YOU BLUR-BLUR pick up this book but acherly dunno what is Singlish, unker will tell you. Singlish is Singapore's unofficial language – because officially we got England, Melayu, Mandarin, and Tamil. Singlish is all these four tok kong languages plus cheena dialects and a few other lingos campur-campur come out one. It is a creative product and hands down the most steady pom pi pi Sinkie invention.

If you think I is biased, I think you should be open-minded. Dun turn into one of those yaya papayas who treat Singlish macam kids' play. Every Singlish speaker knows the type lah. These anyhowly spiak England and then claim they are spiaking Singlish. Their parents last time neh teach them manners one. They bo research but can still see no up cultures they dun unnerstan.

These jokers' knowledge of history oso cannot make it hor. They assume Singlish was from last time our Gahmen made England compulsory in schools and then chewren tombola. But not true lor. Even in the 1970s, Singlish was oredi being analysed at university level. If you go lagi early, the 1950s got young, pandai undergrads experiment and chum-chum local languages to create poetry.

Those budding poets were not stupiak, OK. They knew that, to fight the mental impact of ang moh rule, we in our region must somehow spiak our own way. The power in a language is the power to ownself direct own destiny. So those who think Singlish is all low crass cannot be corright – because got a strand that is quite high crass wor. Oso got a third strand that involves common life, how to friend-friend across cultural divides such as this high-low one.

Language, like life, is always sibeh complex lah. The aim of *The Leeter Spiaking Singlish* is to help show Singlish as not just shiok and sensible but oso intelligent. This book series more or less re-treads my original *Spiaking Singlish* from back in 2017. But that work is so big and fat that some peepur read until peng san. If you suka that book, kum sia – unker suka you back. It remains a kilat testament to what Singlish can do.

But the life of a language must keep moving, and I find changing speowlings and phrasings every now and then quite sian. *The Leeter Spiaking Singlish* is thus my this answer to maintaining a better dynamic form. Other than revising the language and content, I can expand the discussion by chope-ing for each volume a specific category. I can oso add new chapters and make hampalang chapters longer, even double, than before.

The volume in your hands is focus on idioms nia. Simi is an idiom? (I said "idiom", not "idiot" ha.) In the broadest sense, an idiom is a special way of spiaking. Any language with peepur talk cock sing song for a time sure will evolve its own idioms one. An idiom siow-siow uses what is about one thing to describe another thing or it strings words that dun normally connect. We call this use *metaphoric*, and metaphors make communication sibeh stim.

For example, England got this idiom "between the devil and the deep blue sea", corright? The phrase describes a teruk situation where got two courses of action but both kena sai. In Singlish, we may just cowpeh, "Liddis cannot, liddat oso cannot!" But, you see, the very situation got nothing to do with Satan or the sea – unless you an East Coast bomoh. Then OK lor.

But hor – here is the funny part – an idiom may anyhowly, but you the user cannot anyhowly. This is the way. The words are specific and have a specific order, and there is a specific meaning. So, with our England example, you cannot suka-suka go "between the deep blue sea and the devil" or "between Cheng Ho and the Strait of Malacca". You cannot have it describe a banana boat ride either.

This is all unker fewls you need to know now. The other stuff cunning linguists claim to be necessary is really not lah. They just wan to how lian nia. For example, some may insist that an idiom and a metaphor are not at all same-same since a metaphor can still unnerstan if you neh hear it before. You can still gasak buta what. So a poem with a lot of metaphors can work whereas one full of idioms is sibeh jialat.

Others may say an idiom is acherly some sort of fixed expression. They mean a metaphor is a metaphor until everybawdy uses it – then it becomes an idiom. Kong simi? Basically, an idiom is macam an expired or an obiang metaphor, a *cliché*. You the speaker may know what it means but not how come it means that. Maybe it was a joke from your nenek's nenek's time. Or it was a custom peepur forgot about liao.

Debates of this kind can let the lao jiaos ping pong until the lembu thng chu. Only those who jiak pa bo sai pang have the luxury to participate. Unker is personally more interested in a different sort of conversation, in asking what the existence of Singlish idioms must mean. This question is sibeh gerek and can change the way we think about Singlish. Unker will explain why.

First, having an idiomatic dimension means that Singlish is not simper-simper wor. Idioms are not what any Ah Ter Ah Kow can learn with a copy of *The Coxford Singlish Dictionary* (good book!) or Google Translate. You cannot just search what individual words mean and then work out what peepur are saying. Every language tends to transcend the literal and functional, and idioms show how its users chut pattern.

Second, idioms attest to a length of time at play one. They not happening if peepur dun agree on how a group of words must mean a different thing and *that* thing nia. Speakers need to be hiewing one another, talking and listening all the time, in a pally-pally way. The process naturally ties each of them to the spread of the language and oso to its idioms huating.

Third, idioms consperm for us Sinkies that Singlish *is* a language – because why? A language is distinct or unlike other languages only when it got aspects that can get lost in translation. In fact, the harder it is to translate these aspects, the clearer we see got a language in the peektur. Idioms prove how some things just cannot translate word for word one. You can at best favour their meanings over their form or, terbalik, their form over their meanings.

Unker can give you examples. When you hear "itchy backside", most of the time it is not about the ka chng. You can translate into England as agak-agak restless or mischievous or you can say someone is stirring the pot, shit-stirring, or straying from the straight and narrow. Or consider "oon-oon jiak bee hoon". You can replace it with "trouble-free" or "effortless" or you can say "smooth sailing" or "duck soup" or "as easy as pie".

In this volume, I will discuss some chapalang idioms: "balik kampung", "buak gooyoo", "catch no ball", "kiam chye char loti", "potong jalan", "steady pom pi pi", "hentak kaki", "mee siam mai hum", "stunned like vegetable", and "got eyes no see or-yee-or". A lot more idioms will kena mentioned in passing – because Singlish is rich mah! There is no way unker can exhaust the whole catalogue in this leeter book.

Some idioms may be all Melayu or Hokkien, but that does not make them less Singlish hor. Remember how the shiokness lies in their use even by non-speakers of the respective languages. Oso, these idioms may be carrying meanings that originally bo one. So, if you are redi to explore, mai tu liao. Take a dive with me, and hampalang sure will oon-oon jiak bee hoon. Sumpah!

1

WHY "BALIK KAMPUNG" IS RUDE

IDIOMS ARE FUN SIOL! They add colour to a language, and every language in the world got its own truckload of idioms. In England, when you say you let a cat out of the bag, you dun mean you got a bag or a kucing lah. You just mean you are revealing a secret. In Singlish, we would rather say "pecah lobang" – which refers to breaking a hole. This is clearly oso an idiom.

When some ang moh says he missed the boat, nonid to look-see look-see for a sampan – especially when you not near the sea. All he means is he rugi-ed or lost a golden opportunity. But how come this lobang is keem-keem neh? Acherly, it is another idiom. Walao eh.

England is some funny language. To explain one weird phrase, you may have to use another weird phrase.

While idioms cannot be taken literally, the words forming them are not always metaphoric. The kucing let out of the bag may, in fact, be a harimau from a poacher's sack. A refugee maybe got miss a boat... and missed the boat. Context is everything but oso not always, so you must use your brain lor. Someone who is over the moon is confirm-plus-chop not that far off the ground.

Now consider "balik kampung" in Singlish. This translates from Melayu as "go back to your village". It looks macam something literal that, with time, has become metaphoric. We imagine how last time, after zho kang whole day, peepur balik kampung to rilek – so the phrase means thng chu. As in, after I pang kang (not "bangang" ah, which means stupiak), I thng chu. This is what a chunk of younger-generation Sinkies assume.

Except no ler. Nobawdy unnerstans the idiom's sibeh rude meaning better than gila sports fans. These peepur will tell you "balik kampung" cannot anyhowly use one. Not sure if you remember, but, at a SEA Games netball match in 2015, got some of our journalists garang go suan the Malaysian side by cow-pehing "Balik kampung!" The act caused an uproar, which became lagi jialat when the news hit the Malaysian press.

Nanti a bit. Saudara-saudari, can unker take a moment to tolong you? When it comes to friend-friend with another country, can dun go do goondu things and sia suay throw Singapore's face? With a sporting game, whether win or lose, we must always be gracious to our opponents and especially to Malaysians. Malaysians are the only peepur in this big, hostile world who can unnerstan Singlish without being taught – because they more or less spiak like us!

You know what cow-pehing "Balik kampung!" can imply anot? It does not just mean thng chu or translate as "Go and die!" or "Pergi mampus!", as some blur sotongs assume. The real significance is not so straightforward one. If you still gong-gong, must be last time during your geena days you always ponteng inter-school sports meets, corright? Or you would have cow-pehed before lah. No? Dun bedek leh.

The phrase belongs in a competitive or at least an antagonistic setting. It is used as a taunt, a cucuk to rile the other side up. But it does contain buay-songness – so you must not use it to suan an annoying kawan or relative, for example. While the term may seem to originate in some last time inter-kampung games, it is likelier to have emerged from our early years of modernisation.

"Balik kampung!" took off in an era when to ke belakang pusing to kampung life could appear sikit maluating. The homecoming was a loss of face. When you hear the cry "Balik kampung!", it must mean your game performance is so auta that you are better off retreating to your lao, backward home to train some more. Or you can just hide your face and retire – because you totally cannot make it.

"Balik kampung!" was most alive during those heady days of the Kallang Roar. Remember what that phenomenomenon – wah, cheem word – was about? Let us gostan a leeter: the Kallang Roar was not a mall macam today's Kallang Wave hor. Once a pong a time, it involved expressions of a patriotic Sinkie spirit made through kilat cheers for our sportsfolks in the old National Stadium.

But the Roar oso got an ugerly side as captured in three sibeh powderful jeers. Other than "Balik kampung!", there was "Referee kayu!", a cowpeh used to suan a game official thought to be half past six or lazy or unfair. This kayu referee always favoured the opposing team one. "Kayu" means wood, and so "Referee kayu!" is a description of his or her wooden-headedness.

"Kelong!" was the third. A kelong is ordinarily an offshore wooden fish trap cum house for the local fishing folk. Last time got several of them dot our coastlines, but now bo liao. For some reason, Singlish has koped this word and used it to mean tipu-ing or match-fixing. Exactly why saya tak tahu. If someone got a good theory, can share with unker? Issit because the term suggests a man-made platform that can secure advantage for ownself? Or what?

Notice how all three sporty cow-pehs spin metaphors out of last time kampung reality. That lost world had featured attap houses, with many an ayam and anak running about, and a simper-er, less stressful lifestyle. Whether Malaysians still remember anot, those ways of cow-pehing one time united them and us as peepur with shared traditions and unnerstanding. It was how such rustic life-inspired insults could be insults to begin with!

Now, with Singapore completely urbanised, "Balik kampung!" got take a sinister turn and can sound kuai lan in sibeh salah ways. It can come across as xenophobic macam the cry "Go back to your country!" and show us to be hostile and yaya. When hampalang get reduced to identity politics, simi sai, even a football match, can kena politisai one. All that cannot be good for a gamely cucuk.

So, my fellow Sinkies, tolong, OK? Please show some EQ when engaging others lah. Unker is not anti-fun, but, if you must kacau others, be sikit sensitive and dun open mouth anyhowly tembak. Remember how we felt at Suzuki Cup 2021 when that Indonesian captain suanned our Faris Ramli in his face for his penalty miss? Dun liddat lor. Play can play, but dun play-play!

2
WAN TO KENA BUAK GOOYOO?

WHICH GOOD SINKIE does not know punishment? When we small that time, oredi kena caned by our appa amma and, for some of us, by our principals too. Last time we oso kena pull ears and do squats outside classroom at school. Our teachers kokked our heads and niamed our limbs until blue-black blue-black. But last time is last time lah. Now you try doing that and see what happens.

For us men, the pain deen end after adolescence. In the army, we kena drop-twenty plus many times of no-count-start-again and run-and-touch-or-kiss-tree-and-come-back sort of gila-ness. But being civvies oso no fun. We can kena saman for littering lah, jay-walking lah, parking without coupon to have breakfast at the kopitiam lah. During the COVID-19 outbreak, got many kena fined and even jailed for their creative acts of civil disobedience.

In fact, we Sinkies kena punished left, right, centre until "kena" got a higher-order meaning liao. While it works to say "I kena whacked by my ibu" or "I kena tipu by a chow Ah Beng", often you just say "I kena" can oredi. Everybawdy will know you kong simi and commiserate. The implication is that you very the chum, got suffer much, and kena sai, tio bo?

Now, "kena" is a Melayu word that some peepur speowl and pronounce as "kana" because they confuse it with another word in Singlish. "Kena" means being acted upon – but "kana" is Hokkien for like. So "kena sai" and "kana sai" not same-same hor? One means getting shat on while the other means resembling shit. To say your project kena sai or kana sai may be OK, but dun say "I kana sai" when you mean "I kena sai"!

"Kena" is macam "got" in England or "tio" in Hokkien. You can acherly say "He kena hoot!" or "He got hoot!" or "He tio hoot!" – all same-same. In passing, oso please note that "tio" here is not the "tio" of "tio bo" hor. Although both are from Hokkien, the latter is an utterly different word that means corright. Context is important to know if you mean by "I tio" "I kena" or "I is corright".

In Singlish, simi sai you kena for simi reason can use one word to describe: "tekan". "Tekan" means to hurt someone badly or unfairly, and one can be tekanded physically, verbally, or mentally. By the way, the Singlish past participle of "tekan" is "tekanded" because you must stress the lateness in this form mah. So it is "You die", "You died", "You *dieded*". And it is "I unnerstan", "I unnerstood", "I *unnerstooded*".

A physical tekan is macam when a bully hurts a stray kucing because his backside itchy. (Please dun do this, si geenas!) A verbal tekan is kana when a towkay scolds a worker for whole day rileking one corner. A teacher can tekan her students mentally by setting a sibeh siong exam paper. In these first two instances, you can oso use "whack", but you cannot with the third. So mental tekan can be described as tekanning without whacking.

But then there is tekan and there is tekan

– and "buak gooyoo" takes tekanning to a whole teruk level. While anybawdy can tekan somebawdy, not everyone can buak gooyoo, which ordinarily means to spread butter. In Singlish, that is not what it signals at all. Gooyoo-buaking can be done by a powderful source nia, and this tends to mean the state or some law-enforcing agency.

So certain is this fact that, when you use the passive form "kena buak gooyoo", it is unnerstooded who is doing the buaking liao. Oso, "buak gooyoo" is not same-same as "lim kopi", being acherly lagi worse. To lim kopi just amounts to tio called in for – ahem – a drink and a conversation. But to kena buak gooyoo begins with kopi and then gets you so much more. It implies jialat public reprimand or even corporal punishment.

To buak gooyoo is not same-same as to kan or to goreng either. The difference between "kan" and "goreng" is not simply the former, as an F word, is vulgar. To goreng is to tekan long-long while to kan is to do so jialat-jialat. To goreng means to fry in Melayu, but you oredi know this: you got eat goreng pisang and mee goreng mah. In Singlish, gorenging can oso suggest something less scary like suanning.

"Buak gooyoo" is lagi complex because it acherly comments on the victim too. If you kena buak gooyoo, it means you must be guilty of some sibeh salah act.

It oso implies that you must still be kuai lan and go test your luck with the system until you tio your just desserts. (By "just desserts", I dun mean chendol or pulut hitam or cheng tng hor.) So orbigood! There is definitely in "buak gooyoo" this sense of hubris or over-confidence leading to a downfall.

The kua on whom gooyoo is buaked has cucuked too much, has been too garang with being chow kuan. He or she has tempted fate – and so no wonder he or she kena lah! Unker remembers a case back in 1994 of a notti American boi (now not boi liao) named Michael Fay. This ang moh kena caned jialat-jialat by the state for kapo-ing public signs and vandalising cars – and his sentence made Singapore world-famous!

Twenty years later, we got our own si geena in the form of a YouTuber named Amos Yee. While whole Singapore was still grieving over Ah Kong's passing in 2015, this ah boi made a video poking fun at him and Jesus. He deen stop even when he kena buak gooyoo and went on to stir ah stir summore. I remember the whole country getting lagi stressed. That episode we all seriously wan to forget.

The origin of the term "buak gooyoo" is unclear, but unker got hear a few accounts. The most guai-guai account says it came from the England phrase "to be toast", which means you si liao, mampus, habis. When you are told "You're toast!", it means you are in sibeh deep trouble liao. So Singlish speakers just act smart and extend the metaphor by spreading gooyoo on the toast lor.

Another account points to the medical treatment you get after you kena caned in school or prison. This kind of caning is no joke one. After you kena especially by the state, your ka chng will bleed until you cannot sit down for days. You will need to buak koyok, that is to say, apply some quick-fix antiseptic cream – and I dun mean Mopiko or Tiger Balm or tea tree oil hor. I mean something lagi kuat macam Burnol?

Then there is the RA – or adults only – account. This dark version claims the phrase is come from the act of getting it from behind. Yes, it is a reference to male rape in prison siol. In this unnerstanding, the gooyoo is not what you makan for breakfast or use to relieve pain hor. It is what ties "kena buak gooyoo" directly to "tio kan"... but it is kinda sickening lah.

Saya tak tahu if this last account was helped by popular TV crime shows or based on real stories set in Changi one. But those kopitiam Lao Bengs suka arm chio and sumpah it is the true origin of "buak gooyoo". I personally prefer to go with the other two accounts since they fewl likelier in the culture of our conservative silent majority. But, then again, I is very the innocent one.

3

CATCH NO BALL
NO MORE

How come Singlish got so many ways of calling someone clueless ha? Cluelessness is so teruk in Singapore meh? (Nanti, dun answer this question.) There is "blur", which, in England, suggests fuzziness and is used as a noun or a verb. The Singlish "blur" is neither and works as an adjective nia. We Sinkies crown anyone who is always blur-blur a blur king (or queen if char bor).

We oso expand "blur" into the simile "blur like sotong" and the label "blur sotong", both used a lot in the army. Sotongs are squids, but saya tak tahu why we consider squids blur because science acherly says they sibeh pandai one. Maybe it is the way they swim terbalik and macam buay steady? Or, when they tio chuak and gabra, they change colour and chut pattern with inky clouds?

"Gabra" is another word for clueless, and it can be an adjective or a verb. To gabra is to react out of sheer blurness and, in the process, manifest panic. So someone who gabras is a kukujiao who is at a loss and panics and, by panicking, becomes lagi blur. Gabra-ing is such a vicious cycle sial. When you always gabra, you will be crowned as – what else? – a gabra king or queen lor.

The simile form for "gabra" is "gabra like zebra", but dun ask me why a zebra is gabra. I suppose a zebra gabras because "zebra" rhymes with "gabra" – duh? Or maybe a zebra does not know whether it is acherly black on white or white on black? (OK, koyak joke.) Anyway, remember it is "blur like sotong" *but* "gabra like zebra". Dun be that blur sotong or gabra zebra who says "blur like zebra" or "gabra like sotong" ha!

Older generations of Sinkies will know the Cantonese "mong char char", which is sometimes simplified as "MCC" or "MC squared". "Mong char char" oso means clueless – surplise! Unker suka the irony in the form "MC squared" because a fella who is mong char char is anything but an Einstein. Dun you think this contraction is very the pandai? So who says Singlish is stupiak one?

Then there is "cockanathan", which is part-based on either Singlish's "cock", which means rubbish, or England's "cock-up", or both. "Nathan" here is pronounced in the Tamil way ("naa-den") rather than the Judeo-Christian way ("nay-ten"). But please dun listen to those bedek kings and queens who link its origin to our late President S. R. Nathan. No lah! The word has been around for decades and is anyhowly concocted one.

Next, we have the twins "kelam kabut" and "kalang kabut". These are sikit complex because both draw on metaphors. In Melayu, "kelam" means murky and "kalang" dark or blur while "kabut" means fog. So both idioms dun just agak-agak sound the same but oso have the same sense of fogginess. It is hard to know for sure which one came first. No matter lah: whether you kelam kabut or kalang kabut, you are still scrambling amid confusion or luanness.

29

Finally, we come to our champion idiom "catch no ball" – but there is still a hurdle to cross. Its origin got leave many peepur blur since it may be from the Hokkien "liak bo kiew", but *what* is this kiew that is not liaked? Surely, it cannot be a bola linked to the expressions "balls drop", "balls shrink", "bang balls", and "carry balls", where, in all four, balls refer to – RA warning! – testicles.

Both "balls drop" and "balls shrink" mean same-same, which is to be sibeh scared. To bang balls means to be very the frus or anger or geram when things dun work in your favour. To carry balls is almost same-same but different. When you carry unker's balls (metaphorically, OK?), you are doing so to get in *my* favour. So maybe, when you cannot make it carrying balls, you bang balls lor.

"Carry balls" is translated straight from "angkat bola" in Melayu – but saya tak tahu how this idiom came about. You mean got a time when atas peepur need to have their family jewels lifted around one? You ownself use your own imagination lah. If you prefer a more innocent version, Singlish offers you "sar kar" and "tripod", both giving the guai-guai image of three legs.

So what is this bola in a blur sotong's cry "What talking you – I catch no ball"? Or in your date's whisper at some arty-farty performance "Eh, catch no ball"?

The bola here is acherly the common one found in bas-ketball lah, netball lah, volleyball lah, sepak takraw lah, what have you. Such games involve players trying hard to kope a single bola throughout nia.

So what does catching no ball mean but that you sibeh kuniang or you gabra or you out of sync with the game lor. You stretch your hands high in the air to catch a bola you missed or cannot even see! Extend this sense a bit, and the idiom reveals its meaning as getting no meaning. When you liak bo kiew, you are clueless and dunno what the fiak is going on.

My this explanation is no guarantee as I guessbag nia hor. But the idiom does seem tied to another one, "on the ball", which, to be sure, has an England counter-part. Ang mohs say "on the ball" to mean being attuned to new ideas and trends. We Sinkies use it differently to mean sibeh hardworking. So, whenever a MP goes a-visiting HDB blocks, suddenly the grassroots leaders all on the ball one.

"On the ball" can sometimes appear as "on" or "siow on" – literally crazily diligent. "On" should not be confused with "onz", which means something else. "Onz" is to signal your agreement to an appointment or arrangement. So, when you say "Onz!" to running a marathon, you better be siow on about training for it ha. Dun show up on the day and run until balls drop.

Unker connects "catch no ball" with ball games because unker knows last time Sinkies sibeh sporty one. We used to invent and play simper-simper games, and the most gerek one was a ball game called hentam bola. Hentam bola is very the shiok but painful to play. Basically, you take a tennis ball and whack another person with it. The victim groans "Aiyoh! Aiyoh!" and then takes the ball and whacks someone else. This goes on until recess time is over.

What fond memories! Last time, this was how we would friend-friend – in a crucible of mutually inflicted pain that could teach us about life and retribution. Sounds fun anot? Ha, no? What you mean you catch no ball? Kelam kabut and kalang kabut? Mong char char, MCC, MC squared? Gabra like zebra, blur like sotong? You cockanathan geenas nowsaday are just too kuniang to appreciate lah.

4

"KIAM CHYE CHAR LOTI" AND OTHER TRAUMAS

SINGLISH GOT long-long history one! Dun listen to those kuas who whole day talk cock sing song say this say that. They make up all kinds of claims about Singlish macam they lao jiaos. These talk cock kings and queens are sikit different from another kind of royalties, the bedek kings and queens. The latter got talent in bluffing whereas the former can anyhowly pull info out of their ka chng.

So you may hear peepur say we got no Singlish until Singapore became independent. Because last time Sinkies supposedly bo tak chek, England could not have campurred with Melayu and cheena dialects.

Others say Singlish is from low-SES peepur trying to spiak England one. Oso got those who lagi best say Singlish is from Sinkies rebelling against the Gahmen's Spiak Good England Movement.

Wah piang eh! Kawan-kawan, can dun simi sai oso politisai please? Heng our first guru of Singlish, Sylvia Toh Paik Choo, got last time preserve for us some knowledge of how Singlish used to be like. When unker was a geena back in the 1980s, unker got read her solid books *Eh, Goondu!* and *Lagi Goondu!* macam a chow mugger. Many peepur oso did – because they were the national bibles of the time mah.

Toh had wisely gone into her own childhood in the 1950s to unnerstan some of the strange but popular phrases in Singlish. You should really ownself try this if you are a born-and-bled Sinkie lah. Reach into your geena time and dig ah dig. Recall hampalang gila things your ah kong, ah ma, lao peh, or lao bu got say to you and those weird rhymes they got sing during your koon time.

Of course, if your background was ang moh pai one, then kua kua to you lor. Maybe your ah laos sang dunno what "Ding, dong, bell! Pussy in the well!" or "Old MacDonald have a farm". Mine bounced me on their knees and chanted stuff like this:

Fatty fatty bom bom
Malam malam curi jagung
Polis tembak punggung
Jatuh dalam lombong!

The lines mean agak-agak as follows:

Fatty fatty bom bom
Every night goes steal corn
Police shoots him in the back
And he falls into a mine!

Simi sai is this? To be fair, ang moh chewren's rhymes are not any better. I still dunno why Goosey Goosey Gander goes into a char bor's bedroom where got an ah pek he buangs downstairs. Why must Humpty Dumpty sit on the wall and oso fall? And why Jack and Jill go up the hill and fall too? Why yo ah yo a baby on the tree-top until it falls? Why the whole jin gang so accident-prone one?

With our Sinkie song, let us start with that insensitive label "fatty bom bom". A fatty bom bom is an ah pui, "bom bom" being the sound a heavy, wobbly body makes. Yes, the phrase acherly dramatises obesity. It is not nice although we do not know for sure where it came from. The term long-long can find in Caribbean slang and is used in Sri Lanka too. The famous Jamaican reggae singer Carl Malcolm got a song in 1975 called, well, "Fattie Bum Bum".

Nemmind this question of origin. My point here is that we call or used to call peepur that because we learnt from our Pioneer Generation one. That age group might have sacrificed a lot, for which we hormat them forever. They got help Singapore develop and huat through its early decades of luanness and become what it is today. At the same time, they oso got say some pretty sum seng stuff to us, and fat-shaming was one of that.

Summore got criminal allegation in the rhyme! The ah pui sneaks out into the cornfield for a midnight snack... and what happens? He kena shot in the back by the friendly neighbourhood police and falls into a mine. Sibeh tragic ler! How come we were supposed to be entertained? But what to do? Our innocent, leeter heads kena fed this kind of merepek for years, and we deen know better.

The ditty is nonetheless of historical interest because we can see two languages, England and Melayu, campurring! Now I remember another rhyme, a lagi scary one for chewren, that got *three* languages campurring: England, Tamil, and Hokkien. It got geero logic too:

ABC
Kiam chye char loti
Loti bo ho jiak
Ah ma pang sai hor lee jiak!

Here is the rough translation:

ABC
Salted vegetables fried with bread
Bread doesn't taste good
So grandmother shits for you to eat!

What the *fiak*! You are welcome to kiam chye char loti to champion your own take here. "Loti" is a corruption of "roti", the Tamil word for bread, in turn from the Sanskrit "rotika". When my lao bu used to sing these lines to me, it was not to teach me England alphabet but to amuse me during makan. You realise how sick that was? Who got mood for mum-mum when you hear your nenek's shit is oso waiting for you?

Toh's version of this rhyme is sikit different, with just three lines and a different ending. Her last line "Chow sek chow mati" adds Cantonese and Melayu to the mix, making it a ditty with *five* languages! The line means "The moment you eat, you die" – which is not salah since you should neh eat rubbish. Irregardless, it should be clear by now that "kiam chye char loti" means to *make* rubbish.

"Kiam chye" got a meaning other than salted vegetables. It oso refers to being crumpled, as when any paper you whole day keep in your pocket becomes kiam chye. It oso means a mess or a disaster. Thus, if your life has been a series of crises, you can claim to have a kiam chye mia. Just dun confuse "kiam chye" with "chin chye" – which is not even same-same but different? "Chin chye" does not involve vegetables. It just means unfussy.

"Kiam chye" has been around for sibeh long liao. I found it in a notti Chu Chin Chow's mid-twentieth-century poem "Enigma Variations", which lists all the multicultural chio bus around him. Failing to tackle any of them, he says:

Baby, baby
Don't you cry;
Mama, Papa,
Bei kiam chai. [sic]

But "kiam chye char loti" is more than an expanded sense of worthlessness. When someone gasak buta, talks plenty of cock, and ownself cooks up own theory, we say this kukujiao kiam chye char loti. He or she may be a CEO, a political leader, or a top civil servant but is half past six – as good as a chef who fries salted vegetables with bread. Or one of those talk cock kings and queens on Singlish!

5

THOU SHALT NOT POTONG JALAN

We Singlish speakers are very poor things, so you must sayang us whenever you can hor. Some peepur who wan to angkat bola the Gahmen always politisai us and say we sabo England learning. So let me make this clear once and for all. Sinkies should aim (key word) to spiak proper England. In the larger scheme of things, England got more urgent and tok kong uses than Singlish one.

England can help us gain international respect lah, do business lah, make money lah, make more money lah, and so on. There is one other huat peepur tend to forget when comparing, and this is England can at least be lomantic. Singlish is so matter-of-fact that it sounds salah when you use it to tackle someone. Imagine going: "Siti ah, you my chio bu. You so cantik I wan to choot you every day." Cannot make it sial!

No wonder, when it comes to lomance, we ownself declare ownself auta. In fact, in this area, we malu until no steady pom pi pi. Think about it: we Sinkies dun just go pak tor (not parkour) hor. We need to study what we call paktorlogy, the *science* of dating. Science wor, my kawan-kawan! Dating oso must mug? This is what happens when our world-crass education system keeps downplaying the value of the arts.

Paktorlogy refers to a secret body of knowledge our young singles gain access to via the lao jiaos in love. Nobawdy acherly knows the stats for how effective this passed-down knowledge is. But it got codes of behaviour for dating lah, advice on handling what your sayang may say or do lah, where to go lamsing (which is dancing with hugs) lah, where and when to raba-raba lah, whatever.

You say teruk until can cry in the jamban anot? But to pak tor is sibeh susah for us Asians one. Our parents have not prepared us well for this biggest challenge in life lor. That said, the paktorlogy we inherit from them is oso long-long out of date liao. Like you wan to lomance your darling under the moon over satay meh? Besides, if you ask your appa amma, they are likelier to say, "Date what date – go in and study! I catch you sneaking out, I'll piak you ha!"

But there is one kilat code of conduct that has survived every age of paktorlogy, and even young peepur today sappork it. It is this code: "Cannot potong jalan!" What "potong" refers to is not one of those oblong popsicles we last time suka makan hor. That ice cream is made with coconut milk and yam or durian or red bean for flavour and then cut into leeter blocks to enjoy. Shiok!

"Potong" in Melayu means to cut while "jalan" is to walk. To go jalan-jalan means to go for a stroll, which our PM Ah Loong suka and got post about regularly on social media. But "potong jalan" got nothing to do with the same thing done by last time Potong Pasir MP Chiam See Tong hor. By the way, Potong Pasir got its name from its early history as an area with sectioned sand quarries one.

Potong jalan refers to *transgressing*, making a way where there is no way. While this may sound macam something positive and trailblazing, it is acherly not. The kua who cuts and walks is a figure of contempt, a si lang kia, in all of paktorlogy because he or she is being chow kuan. He or she is cutting into another's mating ritual or relationship and kapo-ing another's sayang.

This chow turtle got no honour and is given to his or her carnal nature. He or she bo abide by accepted social rules and thus cannot be trusted. The opposite of potong jalanning in England would be backing off. In Singlish, I guess we could say siam or elak, but those are still not quite it leh. You can still siam or elak and potong jalan what. Maybe berhenti – to come to a complete halt?

If someone is oredi attached, dun go potong jalan lah. You should at most play lamp-post – that is, a supporting role – to that lomance. Dun go steal the limelight or stir ah stir or do some macho or kuniang routine to get attention. You should not be trying to gasak for ownself. That is sibeh ugerly and makes you kiam pah – cannot liddat! Yet, this code has not stopped buayas from doing what they do lor.

Kena potong jalan is among the greatest fears an

ah boi starting BMT can have. This is quite different from his appa amma's greatest fear, which is whether their sayang got makan or tidur enough anot. When the young man is away serving his nation, his chio bu is left open to the pattern chut by kuai lan, opportunistic suitors – and chances are high her heart will kena koped.

Many a chum NS story has revolved around a first love ending liddat one. Many a bad poem has been written about it, and many a goondu recruit has gone AWOL and kena charged because of it. Many a time in the bunks got someone cow-peh liddis: "I will hoot that KNNBCCB who dares to potong jalan my char bor!" But what can he do, really? Bo pian lan lan suck thumb and wait until can book out lor.

The idiom "potong jalan" can be extended for use in any scenario that got some measure of tipu-ing. For example, at the hawker centre, while you are waiting for a plate of sedap char kway teow, some unker may jump queue and potong jalan. At McDonald's, while you doze off in line for your limited-edition Hello Kitty toys, some Ah Lian may cut in and potong jalan.

At work, someone may oso potong jalan your promotion and, with less or no merit, get ahead of you. This last scenario is most shocking as it essentially does not involve jalanning at all. It involves parachuting, being dropped into the game suddenly from

God-knows-where. *That* is super tok kong! When someone can succeed liddat, without need even for the ladder others must use to get to the top, it is truly making a way where there is no way.

6

A STEADY POM PI PI CHAPTER

A FEW YEARS AGO, I might still debate with si geenas over whether it is "steady poon pee pee" or "steady pom pi pi". But now unker lao liao, bo lat liao. So I surrender. You all wan to say "steady pom pi pi", please go ahead. I will sappork you even though you really got no idea where that expression came from. And you know why? Because it is "steady poon pee pee" lah.

To poon pee pee means to blow a whistle in Hokkien. Some say the idiom was popularised by that still act cute TV host Bryan Wong back in the 2000s. Wong certainly got use "steady pom pi pi" a lot in his last time variety show "Steady, Ready, Go!" But my nagging suspicion is that it came lagi early through that funnyman Mark Lee. Who can double-confirm this fewling for me ah?

Oso, normally, Singlish is sibeh minimalist one. We Singlish speakers bo suka use a lot of words when a few can oredi. But here is one of several tok kong instances where that is not true lor. Singlish acherly goes long-long rather than short-short. Last time we would just say "You damn steady!" or "Steady lah!"

– can liao. The point was made and unnerstooded, and everything gao tim.

Singlish's "steady" summore does not denote a lot. It just points to some work being done well, showing brilliance, ability, or promise. To say "Steady lah!" is to consider someone very the capable, very can. It is an encouraging remark. The opposite would be to say, "You cannot make it siol." It thus took a true genius to have convinced us Sinkies that the word "steady" was still not steady enough.

"Steady" in England got a more objective sense in that it generally describes a development. An England speaker may call a gradual, constant, or predictable trend steady. So a financial analyst may repork how a company's investment has been steady. To a Singlish speaker, "steady" is more a personal assessment, tied to perceiving someone as both kilat and zai. It is a balance of competence and character, the mastery of which makes one sibeh champion.

As such, what ang mohs call steady may well not be steady for Sinkies – and the terbalik is true too. Ah Huey may be steadily moving up her career ladder and look every bit a success, but she may not be steady in person. The way she treats others can still be buay zai. Kumar may have a steady love life, but he may not fewl all that steady about it. Maybe he zhngs the lomance too much, acts too much in love, to hide his problems with communication.

As for "poon pee pee", while "poon" means blow, "pee pee" is ono-ma-to-poeic – cheem England word alert! But rilek lah: an onomatopoeia is just a name for something from how it sounds. So, in the scolding "Poot you lah!", "poot" names the magic gas from your lobang where the sun does not shine that goes "poot". "Pee pee", in this sense, got nothing to do with peeing hor. In Singlish, we dun say "I go pee-pee" anyway. It is "I go she-she", another kilat onomatopoeia!

"Poon pee pee" is therefore this image of joy and hope. It is acherly come from an entertainment or sporting context one. Last time, when audience members got excited, they would, of course, clap and shout lah. But they would oso blow leeter, noisy whistles because that was how they released all their pent-up positive energy. So they poon ah poon until they ki siow. It was their way of showing sappork to a performer or a team or just to fewl stim.

That age of gila, ear-pecahing noise pollution was quite something. Unker hopes for civilisation's sake that it is over now although I is not sure whether it still happens. The last time I tuned in to a local TV variety show, I got see a lot of unkers and aunties using long, colourful balloons to clap. Simi sai was that? At least it was considerate, but, as far as idioms go, "steady bob bob bob" not so happening lor.

Where joining "steady" with "poon pee pee" succeeds is in making a speaker fewl song-song gao Jurong. The effect is so shiok that the phrase gets taken into a range of contexts. You can hormat someone for good effort by saying "You very steady leh!" or "Steady poon pee pee!" To spur someone on, you can say "Steady lah!" or just "Steady poon pee pee!" To express your concern, you can say "Steady hor?" or "Steady poon pee pee!"

You get the idea. "Steady poon pee pee" is very the versatile – or should we say very the steady poon pee pee? But there is obviously one more question: how then did we end up with "steady *pom pi pi*" nowsaday? This one is caused by evolution one. Singlish speakers are collectively and unconsciously sibeh creative, and sometimes we do funny tweaks because we are fun and because we *can*.

This is how unker is choosing to explain away something no one knows for certain. It does seem to me that Singlish tends to distort loanwords, words kapo-ed from other languages, to make its own. It may do this by *rounding* sounds, and so "terbalik" became "tombalik", "puncit" "pumchek", and "hentam" "hum-tum". Can blame this trick on ang mohs who taught us to call a pantun "pantoum"?

At this point, some language purists may oredi cowpeh, but, like it anot, that is how language works lah. Borrowed words can change in meaning, pronunciation, and speowling according to their use one. England ownself got a lot of such tweaks: "slogan" came from Gaelic "sluagh-ghairm" and "allowance" from French "alouance". "Lager" was from German "Lagerbier" – but they kapo-ed the wrong word! "Lager" means storehouse, not beer, lah. And how are you saying "homage" and "wanderlust"?

Closer home, Melayu speowls England "taxi" as "teksi", Portuguese "toalha" as "tuala", and Hokkien "diam" as, well, "diam". Mandarin took "bikini" and called it "bǐjīní" (比基尼), "salad" and called it "shālā" (沙拉), and "Coca-Cola" and called it macam "Sedap and Happy" (可口可乐). So, in this case, unker is not fighting it anymore lor. Boleh – "steady pom pi pi" is steady pom pi pi for me!

7
POST-ARMY HENTAK KAKI

THE SINGAPORE ARMY does not turn ah bois to manly men nia. It oso transforms them into Singlish speakers. If a born-and-bled male Sinkie disagrees with this point, chances are he is either a bedek king or the bo zho peng type. Those who got go army will happily tell you their first and *last* time meeting and interacting with the most chapalang range of Sinkies was during NS.

If you got only cheenapok or matrep kakis or are from high-crass ang moh pai, the army sure will set you straight one. From Day One of BMT, you will live and breathe with peepur from across cultural, linguistic, religious, and economic divides. You will learn bits of who they are and how they spiak. The SAF will oso communicate with you in a rojak of England, Melayu, and Hokkien. (Dun ask me why Hokkien.)

No wonder army talk is this sibeh steady source for what ends up in Singlish lah! Its world is not just where Singlish thrives but, lagi shiok, where it gets creative. Guys take common expressions used in their camps balik to their civvie lives and then apply them. To be fair, this is not done consciously hor. You cannot expect peepur to spiak one way for years and then ke belakang pusing when they re-enter society.

Consider how many Singlish expressions are kapo-ed from range practice alone. When your boss tells you to own time own target, what he means is you can do your assignment at your own leisure. Nonid to hurry as got no rules on when to start or finish. But this idiom – sometimes shortened to "OTOT" – came from where one? It is the cue for firers to watch the front, take aim at a target, and shoot when they fewl redi nia.

When you shoot and miss again and again, you will kena branded in army as a bobo shooter. But, when you take too long to pull the trigger, you may be told to take your time instead. In the civvie world, a bobo shooter is someone who a simper task oso cannot do, such as an auta car-parker. "Take your time" is what your boss says when you end up spending too long on your assignment. He wans you to do the opposite, to *not* take your time. Please chop-chop kalipok!

Then there are a chunk of Melayu drill commands that oso get an afterlife. A siow-on colleague (every office got one) may suddenly cow-peh "Sedia!" when a VIP masuks the conference room. Or a supervisor may instruct a cart-pusher to berhenti and unload at a certain spot. "Sedia!" is given to soldiers to get them to look redi while "Berhenti!" gets marchers to halt completely.

"Ke belakang pusing!" is used to achieve an about-turn. When marchers hear this, they stylo-milo move in sync to face the opposite direction and march off. In Singlish, we use "ke belakang pusing" to mean many things from turning tail and cabutting to prata-ing. When you see your ex walk towards you, you naturally ke belakang pusing. A management can oso prata and ke belakang pusing by retracting an unpopular directive.

But the most steady drill-inspired Singlish idiom has to be "hentak kaki". To hentak kaki on the parade square just means to berhenti but not totally. Soldiers still must stamp their feet and so march on the spot. This command makes for a solid metaphor of life moments where you keep moving but go nowhere. In Singlish, we use it on individuals rather than activities, and so a project that kena stalled is more pumchek than hentak kaki.

"Hentak kaki" refers to a fella reaching a point in his or her career where he or she cannot advance further liao. This fate is not because he or she got reach the top but because he or she bo chance to develop anymore. Irregardless of the lumber of years zho kang, the poor thing now has a dead-end job. So, when his or her colleague asks why he or she hentak kaki, it can fewl quite awkward lah.

There are many reasons why peepur hentak kaki, and these may not simply be about qualifications, experience, or competence. Yes, somebawdy could be a blur sotong or a chow kengster at work – in which case he or she deserves to stay put. Orbigood! But it could oso be due to discrimination based on race, gender, age, or whatever. It could oso be because the person is not a white horse.

A white horse is another out-of-army idiom, and it does not refer to a fairy-tale animal hor. It is not Prince Charming's preferred mode of transport and certainly not the rival of a dark horse. A dark horse in England means some unknown kua who somehow manages to get ahead in a task or in life. But a white horse is not unknown one. His or her high-SES or powderful family is, in fact, sibeh prominent.

Soldiers tend to use white horses to explain why some among them are so special. They nonid kena whacked when the whole platoon kena or they can book out when others do guard duty or they can become Occifers. To be sure, the SAF acherly admits got such white horse labels – but their intention is supposed to ensure these atas boi-bois *dun* get special treatment. Saya tak tahu lah.

Suffice to say, when someone hentak kaki, one reason can be that he or she does not have the right connections. This is a mere truth of the real world lor. Indeed, it should now help us see that a lot of army expressions got masuk civvie life precisely because Sinkies find their continued relevance. While army and society are distinct, many challenges, schemes, and patterns still look same-same leh.

Maybe this whole notion of an exit from one life into another is bedek one! Phrases such as "eye power", "Wake up your idea!", and "You think, I thought, who confirm?" continue to describe and address behaviours at work and at home. "Eye power" is a sarcastic reference to watching but bo zho kang. "Wake up your idea!" warns someone to get his or her act together. "You think, I thought, who confirm?" attacks mental complacency.

It is through such application that we manly men demonstrate how we remain thinking soldiers outside of the army. We dun just work macam robots but use our brains to unnerstan and corright social dynamics. Of course, no one says that being pandai must mean being sensitive, and so we suka drag into Singlish all these concepts char bors are blur about. But nemmind! We ownself tell ownself they can own time own target oso learn and use.

8

THAT MEE SIAM MAI HUM MOMENT

SINGLISH ALWAYS kena politisai because Sinkies nowsaday simi sai oso politisai. We say "politisai" rather than "politicise" because that last squeeze on the tongue muscle quite siong leh. Besides, the hard "s" ending got meaning meh? So, instead of "Dun criticise!", we say "Dun critisai!" Instead of "Can subsidise?", we say "Can subsidai?" When we go to our neighbourhood McDonald's , the counter auntie smiles and asks, "Upsai?"

But the "politisai" in the phrase "simi sai oso politisai" is got twist one. It may mean "hampalang gets politisai", but its "sai" is not the same as the "sai" in "eh sai" and "buay sai", that is, can and cannot do. "Sai" in both latter terms denotes ability. The "sai" in "politisai" – despite its gentler tone – invokes shit. So, in "simi sai oso politisai", we acherly got a pun and a rhyme!

You can politisai Singlish and not just *in* Singlish in two ways. One is to do it intentionally, and a good example here involves the idiom "ownself check ownself". The word "ownself" is oredi a kilat Singlish invention! While England got a long-long string of such pronouns – "myself", "yourself", "himself", "herself", "oneself", "itself", "ourselves", "yourselves", "themselves" – Singlish needs one nia: "ownself". Simper.

But, at a 2015 General Elections rally, the Workers' Party's Pritam Singh did something notti. He suanned the ruling PAP Gahmen for claiming to be able to be its own jaga with three words: "Ownself check ownself!" This formulation is sibeh tok kong if you know basic England grammar. The same word is not, in fact, used twice because the first and second "ownself" are same-same but different.

The first "ownself" is an *emphatic* pronoun that means in a personal capacity. The second is a *reflexive* pronoun, with the subject becoming its own object. A close England translation would be, with irony, "I myself check on myself". So the saying does not just chut pattern for the ear but in semantics too. No wonder its first political use blew many Sinkies' minds

and made it an overnight sensation. Waking up one morning, we found it part of Singlish liao.

My this grammar lesson is to helpchoo unnerstan why "ownself check ownself" can mean a lack of accountability nia. Recently, Ministar Ong Ye Kung got try to change its meaning by seeing it as a virtue. He said that, "if ownself cannot check ownself, you're in big trouble". But, in Singlish, being self-accountable should just be "check ownself". While Ong was not salah to prize that, it is not what the idiom means.

The other way to politisai Singlish is cannot plan beforehand one. You just gasak a current political wording and ngeh-ngeh read for irony. This is what happened to slogans such as "cheaper, better, faster", meant to encourage a lean labour force. It has since come to mean to bo hiew workers' condition. "Upturn the downturn" is another one inverted to show how senang it is to talk nia.

The most famous of such politisai-ing got a long but un-un-un-un-un-believable backstory. Unker will tell you, but you must not say I cheong hei hor. During the lead-up to the 2006 General Elections, another WP candidate James Gomez felt buay song because he thought the Elections Department lost one of his application papers. But CCTV footage later showed that – alamak! – he got put it balik into his bag.

This whole wayang was turned into a sibeh funny podcast skit by the gila blogger Lee Kin Mun aka mrbrown. He had a bak chor mee hawker argue with his customer over whether he said he wanted ter kua (or pork liver) anot. We all chio ka peng, but Ah Loong heard oredi not happy. At that year's National Day Rally, he warned such jokers better dun play-play and said, "You put out a funny podcast, you talk about bak chor mee, I will say mee siam mai hum."

Many of us who tuned in to listen that evening were blur siol. You see, "hum" is Hokkien for cockles, and "mai hum" is an instruction to hold the cockles. While we all got PM's point, we oso wondered how come mee siam got hum one. Aiyoyo! Gahmen peepur later claimed PM acherly said "mai hiam", as in "hold the chilli", but we knew what we heard lor. No hum just saying he misspoke mah. I mean harm.

Anyway, the awkwardness made the faux pas lagi famous, and it quickly found use in several contexts. At first, it meant being out of touch, and then it pointed to a political gaffe or any kind of personal blunder. It

now describes this lao kwee situation where one own-self pwns ownself – that is to say, self-sabo. So someone who has to give a business presentation is told not to mee siam mai hum.

There was even a leeter book titled *Mee Siam Mai Hum: The Darnedest Things Singapore Politicians Say*! The brain behind this kuai lan collection of awkward quotes from our own leaders is the publisher Edmund Wee. On Ah Loong's front, he seemed to wan the whole matter scrubbed out, and, for many years, we deen hear officially from that angle again. "Mee siam mai hum" became a folk idiom whose origin most Sinkies have all but forgotten.

That was until National Day Rally 2021 when, out of the blue, Ah Loong said something quite steady pom pi pi. Making his case for higher workers' wages, he said that not just towkays but oso customers should fork out lah. "Pay a little bit more," he says, "for some of our favourite things, like bubble tea or bak chor mee, with or without hum." Wah, everybawdy who heard stunned and laughed until cry.

It was a solid political moment as it cucuked PM's critics who, for years, had thought "mee siam mai hum" proved he bo humour. Now he demonstrated he could ownself laugh at ownself if only to serve the national good. Win liao lor! But then, unker thinks, if he wans to talk about bak chor mee, he should really say ter kua lah. If he wans to talk hum, then it ought to be mee siam. So, on this point, it is still sikit mee siam mai hum.

9

ON BEING STUNNED LIKE VEGETABLE

IF SOMEBAWDY SAYS Sinkies think macam robots, it is a very Sinkie thing to agree. We oso fewl this assessment is bagus what. After all, robots are about technology, and technology is the future mah. Because we suka robots, we tend to confuse this love with an indication of how we think. We assume that, deep inside, we are the law by law, mechanical type. But – aiyoh! – how can this be true?

Just look at our Singlish similes lah. In any language, similes give a good peek into how speakers are mentally wired one. We see how fewlings and behaviours are linked to the big-big world and note the underlying frame of reference. What Singlish similes show is this: Sinkies suka nature a lot! Consider "blur like sotong" lah, "gabra like zebra" lah, "happy like bird" lah, "smelly like shit" lah, and so on.

How do these similes work? Well, I guess sotongs are blur because they swim terbalik and look gong-gong in their inky clouds when they gabra? Zebras gabra for no other reason than "zebra" and "gabra" rhyme? A flying or singing bird easily signifies being free and senang and is not related to a kukujiao no matter what some Lao Bengs say. "Smelly like shit" is nonid to explain one.

All these similes long-long oredi got. They show a peepur's monyet brains that get stim on wild observations. We Sinkies look to nature rather than machines for inspiration even when we and our chewren ki siow over the latest iPhone. Technology may be tok kong, but nature fewls macam a better place to explore our connection to the universe, which is our lives' purpose mah.

But there is one recent simile that is sikit susah to explain lor. The place of "stunned like vegetable" in Singlish is, to be sure, mo tak teng since the day it masuked our vocab. Even its origin is vaguely remembered. Got one time a mock-retro, cheena karaoke song performed by that Lao Beng actor Chen Tianwen went viral. It might be for promoting some TV sitcom called *Spouse for House*, but frankly nobawdy remembers that show lah.

The online music video was a different matter. Who can forget seeing Chen dressed until very the obiang and holding flowers and broccoli as he sang? We all chio ka peng. "Stunned like vegetable" in his mouth just made perfect sense – although what that is remains a mystery. How can a vegetable even be flabbergasted? Where got meaning one? Yet, this is what the image invited us to unnerstan.

STUNNED LIKE VEGETABLE LIAO.

Buang the image, and the meaning should become clear. "Vegetable" refers not so much to a plant as to a human, specifically one whose mind and body bo ho say liao. This sad state is often caused by some kind of brain damage. We do call – although we should not lah – a mental condition with leeter or no response, where one is awake but not fully conscious, a vegetative state.

So when you tio chuak until you cannot spiak or move, you are compared here to having a disorder lor. Yes, this is what "stunned like vegetable" means! So bad, corright? How can be so cek ark? But we Sinkies somehow consider it more funny than horrigible – we are, by nature, not woke one. (Pardon my pun.) We are too kaypoh to be sensitive and suka give peepur stupiak nicknames and ask or talk about their chum-ness in their faces.

As a peepur, we are acherly sibeh jialat. That is why Singlish has the phrase "sorry bo pakay" to express how apologising is useless. "Bo pakay" literally means not valid. Another phrase is "sorry no cure", which highlights how an apology cannot heal the pain. These idioms are used by those we hurt when (or if) we apologise – to remind us next time to think before we say or do something. Not that they have changed anything. Sorry not sorry.

But, looking at the redeeming side of things, we find that "stunned like vegetable" at least got a range of ways to re-frame its meaning. We can, after all, get shocked from being impressed, amused, or scared or fewling buay zai about circumstances. Some auntie can sing so well until we stunned like vegetable. Or she can sing until so teruk that we stunned like vegetable.

In fact, Sinkies get stunned all the time one. We kena a lot of unexpected election results: one time swing one way, next time swing the other way. We kena one time really jialat air pollution from Indonesia and then sudden infection spike for this virus or that virus. In *The Straits Times*, we keep reading of expressway pile-ups or another ti ko male undergraduate in a char bors' jamban. Or we get another stupiak, bo liao forum letter.

To be stunned is acherly a good thing ler. It means that your common sense is still ticking even though your stunned face looks macam a goondu's. "Stunned like vegetable" takes the conventionally zai face of intelligence and *inverts* it to show how Singapore is an irrational, terbalik place. The way to react to ownself thinking ownself smart is to freeze-frame a face of disbelief.

So even an impaired person can give a zhun emotional response to merepek in Sinkie life. This is a point the original music video oso highlights via its other contribution to Singlish, "un-un-un-un-unbelievable". The focus here is the stuttering, leading to the word being sometimes shortened to "un-un-un-un". But what should not be missed is yet another incapacitation being turned into a stunned response.

To illustrate this, say your neighbour's anak suka come to your door and draw ang kong with crayons. You call his amma over, but, instead of disciplining her sayang, she praises his art and remarks, "Lim bu approves!" Your jaw drops, and you diam-diam stare at the two with bak chew big-big. If she still buay unner-stan the whole problem, you hint with the words "I stunned like vegetable".

Or consider how to respond the next time you hear some cockanathan say stuff like Sinkies think macam robots. You can glare at him or her and then freeze until he or she fewls awkward enough to ask if you OK anot. At this point, you spiak in your best C-3PO voice imi-tation, "Robot rosak – because you are too stupiak for words." Watch him or her stunned like vegetable back.

10

WHEN I GOT EYES NO SEE OR-YEE-OR...

"GOT EYES NO SEE OR-YEE-OR" is macam the weirdest Singlish idiom yet. How to even find logic in this construction? The phrase begins with bak chew that cannot see and pratas to a jungle yell. Where is the link between sight or bo sight and cow-peh? What cock is its user trying to express? The whole spiaking sounds sibeh low crass, macam some anak making a first sentence liddat.

But you know what may be lagi worse? Hearing it said in your face. You go to a class reunion where got all your lao kawan-kawan you have not seen in years. Everybawdy talk ah talk about their jobs lah, their spouses and kids lah, on and on. Then it is your turn, and you mention where you tak chek and now zho kang. Hampalang stunned like vegetable. Someone cries, "Wah, Oxford wor! Rajah and Tann wor! We got eyes no see or-yee-or!"

Fewls sibeh eeky, corright? This idiom indeed implies that peepur deen know or have misjudged how kilat or tok kong you are. Maybe you look too modest or low SES or a bit goondu or the kind condemned to a kiam chye mia. But the speaker can oso be a yaya papaya who thinks he or she is sibeh smart and you just kucing kurap. Now this kukujiao must grovel to you in maluation.

Still, this very term is come from where neh? If you are a cheenapok, you can sure guess it is some koyak rendering of the cheena idiom "yǒu yǎn bù shí tàishān" (有眼不识泰山). These words agak-agak translate as "to have bak chew but bo see Gunung Tai". Gunung Tai is the most sacred gunung in China and a UNESCO world heritage site wor. It got shiok historical and cultural significance – but maybe you oredi know from all the wuxia filems.

What this original idiom describes is how, even with your bak chew big-big, you deen know you were in the presence of the lawa-until-cannot-more-lawa gunung siol. The gunung is so big and so famous, and yet your eyesight macam kena sai, so auta until cannot see what is tok kong. So these words are a way to admit or expose a bodoh's presumption. He or she got any-howly see peepur no up and bo show proper respect.

But how then did this idiom *become* Singlish neh? And got difference in use between the two forms anot? Well, you know how it is with Singlish lor. What we borrow will sometimes end up a bit bengkok often for fun. The twist is oso our way of signalling our wish to tweak a bit the context in which these words are to be used. While we suka their idea, yet the meaning buay connect unless it is re-framed.

So, in this case, two things got happen. First is a literal, character-by-character translation – which, to be sure, often comes out quite teruk. The koyakness is a testament of difference and acherly an exersai in self-mockery. But there are times when such translating can work, as when "makan angin" in Melayu became "jiak hong" and "eat air". All three forms, which means to go out for fun, to go kai kai, are used in Singlish.

The second is a pandai play of words. OK, teaching time! The word "homophone" does not describe a kind of phone ha. It is a word that sounds same-same as a different word. So, in England, "our" and "hour" are homophones – and so are "flower" and "flour" (unless

pronounced by Sinkies who go "flaaah"). In Singlish, "amma" and "ah ma", which mean one's abu and nenek respectively, can sound same-same.

Homographs are another thing: they are words that *look* same-same but are acherly different. In England, the verb "lead" and "lead", the metal, are homographs. In Singlish, "mai hiam" is said differently to mean "hold the chilli" or "dun be fussy". Then there are homonyms – which are homophones *and* homographs. These are different words said and speowlt the same way, such as, in England, "pole" as in stick and as in extreme. In Singlish, we got "spiak" as in speak and as in flamboyant.

The original "tàishān" (泰山) oso got a leeter debate relating to homonyms one. Some peepur think it is acherly not a gunung's name but that of some famous carpenter long-long ago. This fella called Tai Shan was kicked out by his shifu Lu Ban, who later found him to be the lao jiao behind some solid furniture lelonging in the market. The episode is even alluded to in Shi Nai'an's classic *Outlaws of the Marsh*.

Singlish treats it as somebawdy's name too, but this person is no carpenter. The homonym is Tarzan in Mandarin. Such a substitution, to be sure, must happen because most Sinkies know a lot of things but not what or where Gunung Tai is lah. Geography is just not islanders' strong suit. When we hear the name, those who can at least spiak Mandarin first think of Tarzan – and that kua we all know.

Once a pong a time, Edgar Rice Burroughs's jungle-raised hero, oso kio John Clayton, Lord Greystoke, was everywhere in mass media one. He got filems lah, TV series lah. His comic strips were serialised in *The Straits Times*, and the ang kong was sibeh cantik. I know because I was one of those geenas who would cut them out religiously and paste in jotter books.

Now, when it comes to personalising something, we Sinkies are sibeh champion. We can connect well with anyone, even an atas ang moh who lives in Africa ler. We just let his gila, primitive but emotional, ape-rousing cow-peh from the screen suck us in. How many of us got monkey see monkey do, imitate Tarzan's cry as we swung on a rope or from bar to bar at the playground or jumped off home furniture!

How quickly that cry became – aiyoh! – a howl of pain as we roll ah roll on the ground. But I bo hear many generations of chewren cow-peh "OOORrr-YYee-eEE-OOR-yEE-EEe-OOORRRR!" liao. For that matter, I bo see peepur siow-siow lift their shirts and beat their chests either. Maybe this is for the better. Got a rhyme we last time used to tease some si geena Tarzan wannabe:

Orr-yee-orr!
Tarzan bo cheng kor!

This second line translates as "Tarzan is not wearing pants" – which is technically true. In other words, we Sinkies may suka play and the wild, but we not stupiak one. We know that Tarzan the hero is ultimately a savage. So "got eyes no see or-yee-or" got one gerek twist to the original, which is that our sucking up is backhanded. The Singlish speaker may acknowledge his or her error of judgement but does not need to see you up. You may be Tarzan, but you still bo cheng kor!

~~GLOSSILY~~ GLOSSARY

Hampalang Singlish words and phrases used in this book are listed here. Those with more than one entry mean they are completely different terms with just the same speowling. Words originating in other languages are given Singlish definitions nia.

ACHERLY: actually
ACT CUTE: try to be funny
ACT SMART: try to be smart
AGAK-AGAK: roughly
AH: and
AH: a filler
AH BENG: uncouth Chinese boy
AH BOI: boy

AH KONG: grandfather; Lee Kuan Yew
AH LAO: adult; senior
AH LIAN: uncouth Chinese girl
AH LOONG: Lee Hsien Loong
AH MA: grandmother
AH PEK: old man
AH PUI: fat person
AH TER AH KOW: Tom, Dick, and Harry
AIYOH: a groan
AIYOYO: a groan
ALAMAK: oh dear
AMMA: mother
ANAK: child
ANG KONG: drawing
ANG MOH: white person
ANG MOH PAI: Westernised class
ANGER: angry
ANGKAT BOLA: ingratiate oneself
ANOT: or not
ANYBAWDY: anybody
ANYHOWLY: anyhow
APPA: father
ARM CHIO: quietly pleased
ARTY-FARTY: keen or active in the arts
ATAS: superior; uppity
AUNTIE: middle-aged woman

Glossary

AUTA: lousy
AYAM: chicken

BAK CHEW: eyes
BAGUS: good
BALIK: back
BALIK KAMPUNG: go home; get lost
BALLS DROP: scared
BALLS SHRINK: scared
BANG BALLS: frustrated
BANGANG: stupid
BEDEK: bluff
BEDEK KING/QUEEN: compulsive liar
BENGKOK: crooked
BERHENTI: halt
BEST: most extreme
BIG-BIG: very big
BLUR: clueless; confused
BLUR-BLUR: semi-consciously
BLUR KING/QUEEN: extremely clueless or confused
    person
BLUR LIKE SOTONG: clueless; confused
BLUR SOTONG: clueless or confused person
BMT: Basic Military Training
BO: without; don't have
BO CHENG KOR: without pants

BO HIEW: disregard

BO HO JIAK: not tasty

BO HO SAY: not in a good condition

BO LAT: feeble

BO LIAO: waste of time

BO PAKAY: invalid

BO PIAN: without choice

BO TAK CHEK: uneducated

BO ZHO PENG: not conscripted

BOBO SHOOTER: incompetent person

BODOH: fool

BOI: boy

BOI-BOI: little boy; son

BOLA: ball

BOLEH: can

BOMOH: shaman

BOOK OUT: check out of camp

BORN AND BLED: born and bred

BRUDDER: brother

BUAK: apply

BUAK GOOYOO: punished

BUAK KOYOK: receive first aid

BUANG: throw

BUAY: cannot; fail to

BUAY SAI: cannot; not allowed to

BUAY SONG: disgruntled

BUAY ZAI: not in control; wobbly

BUAYA: crocodile; flirt

CABUT: run away

CAMPUR: mix

CAMPUR-CAMPUR: mixed; mixing

CAN: capable; good enough; permitted

CAN DUN: can you not

CANNOT MAKE IT: substandard

CANTIK: pretty; lovely

CARRY BALLS: ingratiate oneself

CATCH NO BALL: cannot understand

CEK ARK: cruel

CHAMPION: standout

CHAPALANG: assorted; random

CHAR BOR: woman

CHEAPER, BETTER, FASTER: economically efficient

CHEEM: profound

CHEENA: Chinese

CHEENAPOK: traditional Chinese or Chinese-educated person

CHEONG HEI: long-winded

CHEWREN: children

CHIN CHYE: not fussy

CHIO BU: beautiful woman

CHIO KA PENG: laugh one's ass off

CHOOT: wolf-whistle

CHOP-CHOP KALIPOK: hurry up

CHOPE: reserve

CHOW: smelly

CHOW KUAN: unscrupulous

CHOW MUGGER: disgustingly diligent student

CHOW TURTLE: disgusting person

CHUM: miserable

CHUM-CHUM: mix

CHUM SIONG: negotiate

CHUT PATTERN: resort to tricks

CIVVIE: civilian

COCK: nonsense

COCKANATHAN: nonsense; idiot

CONFIRM-PLUS-CHOP: guaranteed

CONSPERM: confirm

CORRIGHT: correct

COW-PEH: shout

CRITISAI: criticise

CUCUK: taunt

CUM: and

DEEN: didn't

DIAM: keep quiet

DIAM-DIAM: quietly

DIEDED: died (past participle)

DOUBLE-CONFIRM: re-confirm

DUH: dull-witted

DUN: don't

DUN LIDDAT: don't behave this way

DUN PLAY-PLAY: don't fool around; don't underestimate

DUNNO: don't know

EAT AIR: go for a ride

EEKY: unnerving

EH: a filler

EH SAI: can; allowed to

ELAK: avoid

ENGLAND: English

EVERYBAWDY: everybody

EXERSAI: exercise

EYE POWER: reluctance to act or participate

FATTY BOM BOM: fat person

FEWL: feel

FEWLING: feeling

FILEM: film

FRIEND-FRIEND: make friends

FRUS: frustrated

GABRA: panic

GABRA KING/QUEEN: extremely panicky person
GABRA LIKE ZEBRA: panic
GAHMEN: government
GAO TIM: settled
GARANG: brave
GASAK: grab
GASAK BUTA: make wild guesses
GEENA: child
GEERO: zero
GERAM: resentful
GEREK: awesome
GILA: crazy
GO AND DIE: get lost
GONG-GONG: ignorant
GOONDU: idiot
GOOYOO: butter
GORENG: fry
GOSTAN: reverse
GOT EYES NO SEE OR-YEE-OR: be blind to the fact
GUAI-GUAI: obedient
GUESSBAG: make wild guesses
GUNUNG: mountain

HA: for expressing caution
HABIS: finished
HALF PAST SIX: lackadaisical

HAMPALANG: all

HAPPENING: fashionable

HAPPY LIKE BIRD: chirpy; contented

HARIMAU: tiger

HDB: Housing and Development Board

HELPCHOO: help you

HENG: lucky

HENTAK KAKI: cannot advance

HENTAM: whack

HIEW: regard

HIGH CRASS: high class

HIGH SES: high socio-economic status

HOOT: beat up

HOR: for reminding or expressing irritation

HORMAT: salute

HORRIGIBLE: horrible and incorrigible

HOW LIAN: boast

HUAT: gain; prosper

HUM-TUM: whack

IBU: mother

IRREGARDLESS: regardless

ISSIT: is it

ITCHY BACKSIDE: restless; mischievous

JAGA: guard

JALAN: walk

JALAN-JALAN: a stroll

JAMBAN: toilet

JIAK HONG: go for a ride

JIAK PAH BO SAI PANG: pointlessly engaged

JIALAT: terrible

JIALAT-JIALAT: a serious extent

KA CHNG: backside

KACAU: irritate

KAI KAI: go out for leisure

KAKI: buddy

KALANG KABUT: panic

KAMPUNG: village

KAN: f**k; scold

KANA: like

KAPO: grab

KAWAN: friend

KAWAN-KAWAN: friends

KAYPOH: busybody; meddle

KAYU: incompetent

KE BELAKANG PUSING: turn around

KEEM-KEEM: golden

KELAM KABUT: panic

KELONG: cheat

KENA: get

KENA SAI: get shat on

KENGSTER: skiver

KI SIOW: go crazy

KIAM CHYE: crumpled

KIAM CHYE CHAR LOTI: make a mess

KIAM CHYE MIA: worthless life

KIAM PAH: deserve a beating

KILAT: excellent

KIO: known as

KNNBCCB: a vulgarity

KOK: hit

KONG SIMI: what do you mean

KOON: sleep

KOPE: capture

KOPI: coffee

KOPITIAM: coffeeshop

KOYAK: damaged; inferior

KOYOK: medicine

KUA KUA: a sigh of disappointment

KUA: fool; clown

KUAI LAN: rascally

KUAT: strong

KUCING: cat

KUCING KURAP: insignificant

KUKUJIAO: idiot; rascal

KUM SIA: thank you

KUNIANG: feminine

LAGI: even more
LAGI BEST: incomparable
LAH: for emphasis or enumeration
LAMP-POST: supporting figure
LAMSING: hugging and dancing
LAN LAN: grudging
LAO: old
LAO BENGS: uncouth Chinese men
LAO BU: mother
LAO JIAO: old hand; expert
LAO KWEE: embarrassing
LAO PEH: father
LAST TIME: long ago; at one time
LAST TIME IS LAST TIME: what is past is past
LAW BY LAW: by the book
LAWA: gorgeous
LEETER: little
LEFT, RIGHT, CENTRE: everywhere
LEH: come on
LELONG: on sale
LEMBU: cattle
LER: do you know
LIAK BO KIEW: cannot understand
LIAO: already; finished

LIDDAT: like that

LIDDIS: like this

LIM: drink

LIM BU: female first person

LIM KOPI: face interrogation

LOBANG: hole; opportunity

LOMANCE: romance

LOMANTIC: romantic

LONG-LONG: very long; long ago

LOOK-SEE: survey

LOR: for expressing resignation

LOSE FACE: be humiliated

LOTI: bread

LOW CRASS: low class

LOW SES: low socio-economic status

LUAN: chaotic

LUMBER: number

MACAM: like

MAH: don't you know

MAI HIAM: don't be fussy

MAI HIAM: hold the chilli

MAI HUM: hold the cockles

MAI TU LIAO: don't wait any longer

MAKAN ANGIN: go for a ride

MAKAN: food; eat

MALU: embarrass; embarrassing

MALUATING: embarrassing

MALUATION: embarrassment

MAMPUS: die

MASUK: enter

MATI: die

MATREP: wayward Malay boy

MC SQUARED: clueless or confused

MCC: clueless or confused

MEE SIAM MAI HUM: a glaring blunder

MEH: for expressing doubt

MELAYU: Malay

MEREPEK: nonsense

MINISTAR: minister

MO TAK TENG: incomparable

MONG CHAR CHAR: clueless; confused

MONKEY SEE MONKEY DO: copy without thinking

MONYET: monkey; troublemaker

MUG: study

MUM-MUM: food

NANTI: wait

NEH: what about

NEH: never

NEMMIND: never mind

NENEK: grandmother

NGEH-NGEH: persistently

NIA: only

NIAM: pinch

NOBAWDY: nobody

NONID: no need

NOTTI: naughty

NOWSADAY: nowadays

NS: National Service

OBIANG: out of fashion

OCCIFER: army officer

OK LOR: if you say so

ON: hardworking and motivated

ON THE BALL: hardworking and motivated

ONCE A PONG A TIME: once upon a time

ONE TIME: once

ONZ: we have an agreement

OON-OON JIAK BEE HOON: smooth sailing

ORBIGOOD: serve you right

OREDI: already

OSO: also

OTOT: own time own target

OWN TIME OWN TARGET: at your convenience

OWNSELF CHECK OWNSELF: unaccountable

OWNSELF PWN OWNSELF: self-sabotage

OWNSELF: on one's own; personally

PAK TOR: dating

PAKTORLOGY: advice on dating

PALLY-PALLY: on friendly terms

PANDAI: clever

PANG KANG: finish work

PANG SAI: take a dump

PANTOUM: a Malay verse form

PANTUN: a Malay verse form

PAP: People's Action Party

PARACHUTE: appoint an outsider to high office

PECAH: break; broken

PECAH LOBANG: wreck a scheme

PEEKTUR: picture

PEEPUR: people

PENG SAN: faint

PERGI MAMPUS: get lost

PIAK: slap

PING PONG: to and fro

PIONEER GENERATION: wartime generation of
    Singaporeans

POLITISAI: politicise

PONTENG: play truant

POON: blow

POON PEE PEE: whistle

POOT: fart

POOT YOU: an angry interjection

POTONG: cut; ice cream

POTONG JALAN: steal someone's lover; jump queue

POWDERFUL: powerful

PRATA: flip-flop

PUMCHEK: exhausted; deflated

PUNCIT: punctured

RA: adults only

RABA-RABA: grope

REDI: ready

REPORK: report

RILEK: relax

ROJAK: mix

ROSAK: broken

ROTI: bread

RUGI: lose

SABO: sabotage

SAF: Singapore Armed Forces

SAI: shit

SALAH: wrong

SAMAN: summons

SAME-SAME: alike

SAME-SAME BUT DIFFERENT: superficially alike

SAMPAN: boat

SAPPORK: support

SAR KAR: ingratiate oneself

SAUDARA-SAUDARI: brothers and sisters

SAYA TAK TAHU: I don't know

SAYANG: love; cherish; empathise with; wasteful

SEDAP: delicious

SEDIA: stand at attention

SEE NO UP: look down on

SENANG: easygoing

SHE-SHE: pee

SHIFU: master

SHIOK: amazing

SHORT-SHORT: very short

SI GEENA: brat

SI LANG KIA: bastard

SI LIAO: this is doomed

SIA SUAY: be an embarrassment

SIAL: for expressing incredulity

SIAM: move aside

SIAN: boring

SIBEH: very

SIKIT: a little

SIMI: what

SIMI SAI: whatever matter

SIMI SAI OSO POLITISAI: politicise anything and
    everything

SIMPER: simple

SIMPER-SIMPER: very simple

SINKIE: Singaporean

SIOL: for expressing incredulity

SIONG: tough

SIOW: crazy

SIOW-SIOW: fool around; thoughtlessly; funnily

SIOW ON: irrationally or excessively motivated

SMELLY LIKE SHIT: very smelly

SOLID: outstanding

SOMEBAWDY: somebody

SONG-SONG GAO JURONG: feel good all the way

SORRY BO PAKAY: too late for an apology

SORRY NO CURE: too late for an apology

SORRY NOT SORRY: insincere apology

SOTONG: squid

SPEOWL: spell

SPEOWLT: spelt

SPIAK: speak

SPIAK: flamboyant

STEADY: impressive

STEADY POM PI PI: well done

STEADY POON PEE PEE: well done

STIM: stimulating

STIR AH STIR: provoke

STUNNED LIKE VEGETABLE: dumbfounded

STUPIAK: stupid

STYLO-MILO: stylish

SUAN: taunt

SUBSIDAI: subsidise

SUCK THUMB: be helpless

SUKA: like

SUKA-SUKA: as one pleases

SUM SENG: crazy

SUMMORE: some more

SUMPAH: swear; promise

SURPLISE: surprise

SUSAH: difficult

TACKLE: woo

TAK CHEK: study

TAKE YOUR TIME: don't take your time

TALK COCK: talk nonsense

TALK COCK KING/QUEEN: extremely nonsensical
    person

TALK COCK SING SONG: talk nonsense

TEKAN: pressure

TEKANDED: pressured (past participle)

TEMBAK: shoot

TERBALIK: the other way round

TERIMA KASIH: thank you

TERUK: nasty; tough

THNG CHU: go home

THROW FACE: embarrass

TI KO: lecher

TIDUR: sleep

TIO: get

TIO BO: am I right

TIO CHUAK: shocked

TIPU: trick; cheat

TOK KONG: important

TOLONG: a plea for help

TOMBALIK: the other way round

TOMBOLA: randomise

TOWKAY: boss

TRIPOD: ingratiate onself

UGERLY: ugly

UN-UN-UN-UN: extremely difficult to believe

UN-UN-UN-UN-UNBELIEVABLE: extremely difficult to believe

UNKER: middle-aged man

UNNERSTAN: understand

UNNERSTOODED: understood (past participle)

UPSAI: upsize

UPTURN THE DOWNTURN: change a situation for the better

USE YOUR BRAIN: put in some thought

VANAKKAM: hello
VERY THE: very

WAH PIANG EH: for goodness's sake
WAH: a cry of wonder
WAKE UP YOUR IDEA: take matters seriously
WALAO EH: for goodness's sake
WAN: want
WAYANG: staged performance
WHACK: beat up; apply
WHAT TALKING YOU: what do you mean
WHAT THE FIAK: what the f**k
WHITE HORSE: someone with a rich or influential
    background
WHOLE JIN GANG: everyone involved or affected
WIN LIAO LOR: you are unassailable
WOR: for expressing surprise
WORLD-CRASS: world-class

YAYA: arrogant; aloof
YAYA PAPAYA: arrogant person; show off
YO AH YO: cradle
YOU THINK, I THOUGHT, WHO CONFIRM: what is
    the basis for saying so

ZAI: cool

ZHNG: embellish

ZHO BO: do nothing

ZHO KANG: work

ZHUN: accurate

ABOUT THE AUTHOR CUM ILLUSTRATOR

Gwee Li Sui suka write lah, draw lah, talk cock sing song lah. He got publish many kilat books from poetry books and comic books to critical guides and lite-ra-ry anthologies. You got buy any of those? Bo, corright? That is why he must now oso make Singlish books lor. Other than *Spiaking Singlish*, he got translate world classics into Singlish, such as Antoine de Saint-Exupéry's *The Leeter Tunku*, Beatrix Potter's *The Tale of Peter Labbit*, and the Brudders Grimm's fairy tales. This unker sibeh siow on one!